TH — N

THE ? NL ND

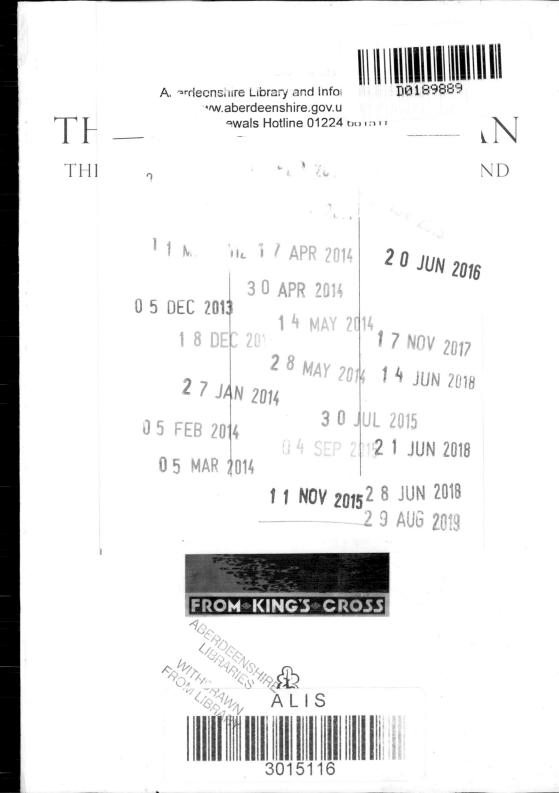

FROM KING'S CROSS

Published in Great Britain in 2010 by Shire Publications
Ltd, Midland House, West Way, Botley, Oxford OX2 0PH,
United Kingdom.
44-02 23rd Street, Suite 219, Long Island City, NY 11101
E-mail: shire@shirebooks.co.uk   www.shirebooks.co.uk

Every attempt has been made by the Publishers to secure
the appropriate permissions for materials reproduced in
this book. If there has been any oversight we will be happy
to rectify the situation and a written submission should be
made to the Publishers.

A CIP catalogue record for this book is available from the
British Library.

Shire Library no. 586   •   ISBN-13: 978 0 74780 770 4

NMSI Trading Ltd has asserted its right under the
Copyright, Designs and Patents Act, 1988, to be identified
as the copyright holder of this book.

Designed by Tony Truscott Designs, Sussex, UK
and typeset in Perpetua and Gill Sans.
Printed in China through Worldprint Ltd.

10 11 12 13 14   10 9 8 7 6 5 4 3 2 1

COVER IMAGE
In this unusual poster the locomotive *Flying Scotsman*, in
'British Empire Exhibition' condition, is used as a symbol
of the speed, power and glamour of the LNER's principal
expresses, with the potential to link passengers to the
world via the great passenger liners of the day.

TITLE PAGE IMAGE
By the 1930s the Flying Scotsman service was famous
enough for the name to be evoked simply by a large wing
shape, as in this poster by Freiwirth.

CONTENTS PAGE IMAGE
Great Northern Railway locomotive 773, pictured around
1900. These locomotives, designed by Patrick Stirling,
were capable of speeds of up to 85 mph and helped
establish a reputation for speed on the East Coast Main line
between London and York.

THE NATIONAL RAILWAY MUSEUM
The National Railway Museum, York is the largest railway
museum in the world. Its permanent displays and
collections illustrate over 300 years of British railway
history, from the Industrial Revolution to the present day.
The Flying Scotsman locomotive was acquired by the
museum in 2004 and forms part of the National
Collection. The NRM archive also includes a fabulous
collection of railway advertising posters charting the
history of rail. Visit www.nrm.org.uk to find out more.

This book is produced under licence from National
Museum of Science and Industry Trading Limited.
Royalties from the sale of this book help fund the National
Railway Museum's exhibitions and programmes. The
National Railway Museum Collection is a registered
trademark, no. 2309517.

All images are courtesy of National Railway Museum/
Science and Society Picture Library, except for the
following, which are reproduced by kind permission of:

John Allison, page 54; Gresley Society, page18;
James A. Brown/The Gresley Society, page 46;
Robert Gwynne, page 53; Roland Kennington, page 52
(bottom); Robin Patrick, page 52 (top); Davina Pike,
page 50 (bottom); private collection, pages 10 (bottom)
and 23 (top); N. Townend Collection, page 19 (top);
Trustees of the Royal Air Force Museum, page 29.

Shire Publications is supporting the Woodland Trust, the UK's leading woodland conservation charity, by funding the dedication of trees.

CONTENTS

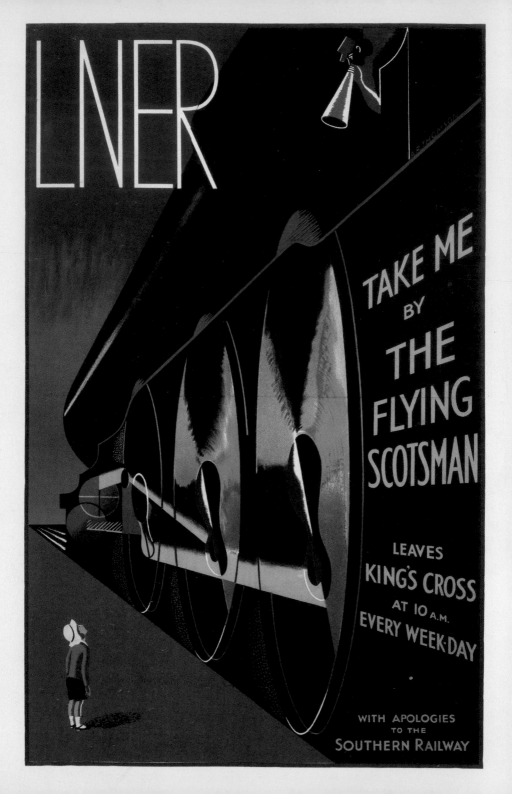

THE EMPIRE FINDS A STAR

IN DECEMBER 1923 an almost brand new express locomotive, with the number 1472, was returned to Doncaster works for a complicated repair. A crucial component – the centre piston rod – had fractured. At the same time, in London, final arrangements were being made for the British Empire Exhibition, a giant promotion for the industries and artistic endeavours of Britain's sprawling Empire. It was to be the largest exhibition ever conceived, and the destination for over 26 million visitors. The Palace of Engineering, at that time the largest concrete structure in world, would include exhibits featuring Britain's railways, and the newly formed London and North Eastern Railway (LNER) was very keen to benefit from the publicity it would bring.

Two major stars would emerge from the exhibition. The first was the Empire Stadium, which became the spiritual home of football, Wembley. The second was a railway engine. Selected because of the fault that had taken it out of revenue-earning service, class 'A1' Pacific number 1472 would fly the flag for the LNER. Long, lithe and handsome, it was a design that combined grace and power, and it was the perfect advertisement for the new railway company that aspired to be the best in the land. It was prepared to a showroom finish of apple green, its cabside was adorned with the company's crest, and it was wrapped up and sent to London.

The locomotive would be used to promote the railway company's most famous train – the service between London and Edinburgh that left each city at 10 a.m. every day. For years this train had been popularly known as 'The Flying Scotsman', and now the LNER decided to capitalise on this. The 'Flying Scotsman' name was given official sanction and the show-stopping locomotive (now renumbered 4472) was named *Flying Scotsman* in honour of what the company declared to be 'the most famous train in the world'. It became a sensation, and its name entered the popular vocabulary.

More than eight decades of publicity about the train service have built up not a little confusion, as both are known as the Flying Scotsman. This is the story of a famous train, and of the locomotive which became a star in 1924 and has remained one ever since.

Opposite:
The 1932 speed up of the Flying Scotsman service was promoted by this poster by A. R. Thompson. Influenced by the art of the 'Futurists' the design also borrowed from a famous Southern Railway poster. Not popular with the public at the time, the design was not re-issued.

5

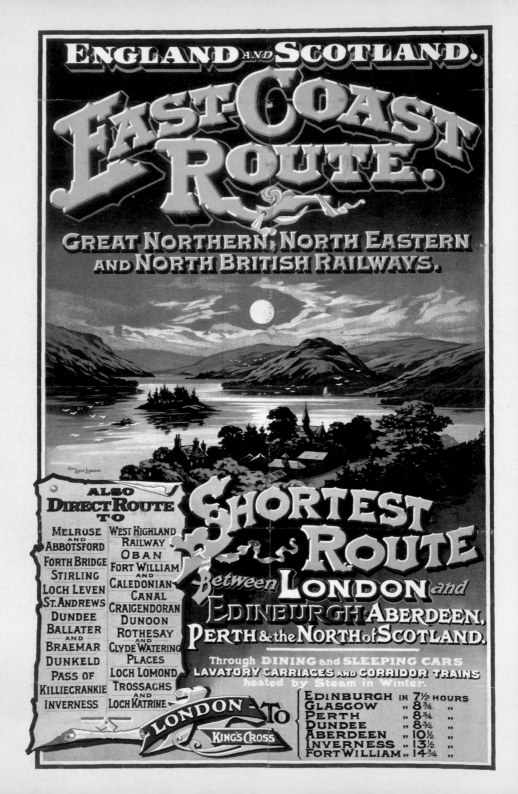

SPEED TO THE NORTH

BEFORE the nineteenth century, people travelling between London and Edinburgh went either along the Great North Road or, more frequently, by sea. By the late eighteenth century a stagecoach service was available once a month and the journey took a fortnight, 'if the weather [were] favourable'. By 1848 there were railways and one could travel the whole way by train along what is now called the West Coast Main Line, from London Euston to Edinburgh in a mere twelve and a half hours.

Taking a train from London to Edinburgh via York and Newcastle had to wait a little longer as the crossings of the Tyne and Tweed required major bridges. However, by 1850 passengers for Scotland could travel between London and Edinburgh along a route similar to that of the old Great North Road, and by 1852 they could depart from the Great Northern Railway's new London station at King's Cross. In Edinburgh passengers arrived at Waverley station, although today's grand station (an amalgamation of three previous ones) was not built until 1868. Almost immediately, there was a 'Scotch Express' available, leaving King's Cross at 7.40 a.m. and arriving in York over seven hours later, to give a connection to Edinburgh. By 1855 the train included through carriages, enabling passengers to travel the whole distance without changing trains.

In 1860 Walter Leith, General Passenger Superintendent of the Great Northern Railway (GNR), suggested that the three companies that operated the East Coast route (the GNR, the North Eastern Railway and the North British Railway) share the cost of building new coaches for through trains. The Great Northern, which had already gained a reputation for comfort and speed, wanted to ensure the lucrative through trade was run to their standards. The result was the East Coast Joint Stock Company (ECJS), with new carriages for the 'Scotch Express' being built by the GNR at Doncaster.

In June 1862 a new service between London and Edinburgh was begun. Departing from London King's Cross going north and from Edinburgh Waverley going south at 10 a.m., this was to be the East Coast route's principal daytime train, and it has remained so ever since. It was referred to

Opposite:
This poster, produced in the year of the 1895 'Races to the North', shows the joint working arrangements by the Great Northern Railway (GNR), the North Eastern Railway (NER) and the North British Railway (NBR) which collaborated to provide the East Coast Joint Stock 'lavatory carriages and corridor trains'.

in Bradshaw's railway timetable as the 'Special Scotch Express'. It took only ten and a half hours, including half an hour at York for lunch. Up and down the line railwaymen, rail users and railwayacs (the early name for railway enthusiasts) started referring to this train as the 'Scotch Express', the 'Scotchman' or, using the language of the stagecoach era, the 'Flying Scotchman'.

Fading memories of stagecoaches bumping along at 12 mph and experience of the North British Railway's poor-quality coaches meant that carriages of the East Coast Joint Stock, capable of smooth running at 40 mph, were a revelation. By today's standards, passenger accommodation was spartan but it reflected what had gone before, with provision for the hire of rugs and foot-warmers (carriages being unheated), and oil lamps for when it got dark. When in 1877 the Glasgow & South Western Railway introduced padded seat backs in third class, this innovation was resolutely opposed by the North Eastern Railway for East Coast Joint Stock coaches. But this typical piece of Victorian conservatism did not affect passengers on the 10 a.m. — this train, which catered only for wealthier travellers, carried only first- and second-class passengers at this time. Third-class passengers would have to wait until 1887 to take the 'Scotchman' to Edinburgh.

Lavatories were not provided, the stops for the engines to take water or to be changed (as horses had been in stagecoach days) being regarded as giving passengers sufficient time for their needs. Peterborough, one of the

A busy King's Cross station in August in the late nineteenth century, as friends gather to head north for the grouse-shooting season, with East Coast Joint Stock coaches in the background. George Earl, who painted this picture in 1893, was famous for his animal studies — hence the large numbers of dogs in the painting.

main stations where operating requirements (a change in locomotive or a stop for water) gave sufficient time for those in the know, was regularly the scene of a rush of passengers to the refreshment room. However, in the days before disposable cups, hot drinks had to be consumed on the premises.

At York a half-hour break for lunch was available, although here the suspicion was that the scalding temperature of the soup was to prevent passengers finishing their meal before the whistle for departure, enabling food left behind to be sold to someone else! It took until 1883 before the ECJS trains featured corridor coaches with heating and on-train lavatories, although even then not every carriage was this up-to-date. The introduction of corridor coaches for the whole train allowed the lunch stop at York to be dropped in 1900.

Whilst the Great Northern revelled in its reputation as the company with the fastest trains in Britain, for many years its locomotives and carriages did not have an effective automatic brake, and emergency braking procedure often meant putting the engine into reverse. This was highlighted in the Abbots Ripton crash in 1876 when fourteen people on the 'Scotch Express' were killed and the Board of Trade insisted on improvements.

Rivalry with the West Coast route started early and a 10 a.m. departure from London Euston for Edinburgh was soon in Bradshaw's railway timetables.

From the 1870s up to the turn of the twentieth century the '10 a.m.' was hauled between London and York by Patrick Stirling's legendary 'Singles'. This photograph shows number 221, built in 1876, at the head of a train newly arrived at King's Cross from the north around 1890.

The interior of a third-class carriage built for the East Coast Joint Stock in 1895.

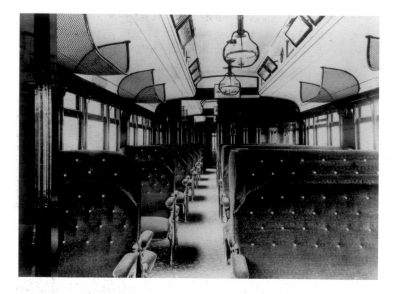

When in June 1888 the East Coast companies advertised a time of nine hours for the journey and admitted third-class passengers to the train, the West Coast route had to respond. The result was the 'Railway Races' between the rival routes, with carefully arranged engine changes and shorter trains helping to accelerate the fastest services. By August, on the East Coast route the 'Scotchman' had achieved a time of 7 hours and 27 minutes for the whole run, a good three hours quicker than in 1862. This trip was reported to have been inclusive of the lunch stop at York and 'a delay caused waiting for a hay barge to clear the River Ouse at Selby Swing Bridge'.

North of York, East Coast expresses were handled by locomotives of the North Eastern Railway. This coloured postcard view shows an express train of ECJS carriages – probably the 'Flying Scotsman' – behind a pair of NER 4-4-0 locomotives around 1900.

East Coast Express N.E.R.

This 'Race to the North' certainly grabbed the headlines but the special arrangements cost the companies money and the 'racing', though good for publicity, was potentially dangerous. By August the rival companies had agreed to stop racing and stick to a minimum time for the journey from

A poster from 1900 promoting the East Coast Main Line as the 'shortest and quickest' route to a number of principal Scottish destinations. It shows how the three companies that ran the route were able to make the most of their arrangements for expresses on the line.

A postcard from the early 1900s shows the 'Flying Scotsman' passing Hadley Wood, north of London, hauled by an Ivatt 'Atlantic', the kind of locomotive that A1 *Flying Scotsman* was designed to replace.

THE "FLYING SCOTSMAN" PASSING HADLEY WOODS.

The North Eastern Railway also built 'Atlantics' for use on heavy East Coast passenger trains. This coloured postcard shows Class V locomotive number 794 departing Edinburgh Waverley with an express bound for London at the end of the Edwardian period.

London to Edinburgh. A time of eight and a quarter hours for express trains between the two capitals was to be kept in place long after the locomotives and carriages were capable of a much faster time. Even another bout of racing, prompted by the opening of the direct route to Aberdeen in 1895, was soon called to a halt and the time agreed in 1888 retained. As one historian was to quip, by the time the agreement was broken in 1932, dead fish landed at Aberdeen for the London fish market often travelled faster than passengers on an East Coast route express.

By 1892 the *Strand* magazine was referring to the East Coast service as the 'Flying Scotchman', and in the same year a dining car was provided for the first time for first-class passengers. In 1893 the *Railway News* referred to the train as the 'Flying Scotsman' although it would be thirty years before it was officially called this. In 1906 the King Edward Bridge in Newcastle was built and for the first time through trains on the East Coast route no longer needed to reverse on their journey north (the through station at York had opened in 1877).

Corridor carriages and restaurant cars made for heavier trains than hitherto, and more powerful engines were needed if the cost of using two engines ('double-heading') was to be avoided. In 1898 the GNR's Henry Ivatt introduced the first of his powerful 'Atlantic' locomotives, capable of hauling much heavier trains than the engines they replaced. Hence, when the GNR recruited the young and innovative Nigel Gresley to head their carriage and wagon department in 1905, improvements could continue.

Gresley would in time introduce to the Anglo-Scottish service a range of innovative features such as 'pressure ventilation' (a kind of early air-conditioning), electric cookers in the dining cars (much safer than the gas cookers they replaced), and attention to the wheels and frames on which the carriages sat, ensuring comfort at high speed. However, it would be when he succeeded Ivatt and started designing locomotives that Gresley would achieve lasting fame and the route become established in the public's mind as 'the route of the Flying Scotsman'.

Over fifty years of express locomotive power on the Great Northern Railway is represented in this illustration showing Stirling 'Single' number 1 of 1870 (preserved by the GNR in 1907) alongside A1 *Sir Frederick Banbury*, sister engine to *Flying Scotsman*, and which entered service in July 1922.

NIGEL GRESLEY: 'KNIGHT OF THE IRON ROAD'

IN 1893 Herbert Nigel Gresley, the son of a vicar and of aristocratic lineage, left Marlborough College. He became a 'premium apprentice', not at the nearby Swindon works but at Crewe, then a powerhouse of locomotive experimentation.

Under the difficult but innovative Francis Webb, Chief Mechanical Engineer of the London & North Western Railway, Gresley would acquire a wide range of skills. As an apprentice at Crewe, he witnessed the second 'Race to the North' in 1895, a press sensation and an exciting time for budding engineers like Gresley. Crewe was to prove the springboard for a wide-ranging railway apprenticeship. Gresley moved from there to the Lancashire & Yorkshire Railway (L&YR) and soon found himself testing materials at Horwich, near Bolton, before a summer working as the running shed foreman at Blackpool. He was to retain a lifelong appreciation of scientific testing, and for the work of enginemen.

In 1902, the year that the football team that had started at the L&YR's Newton Heath carriage and wagon works became Manchester United, Gresley was appointed works manager at Newton Heath. Recently married and now earning an annual salary of £250, the 'Great White Chief', as he was later sometimes called, was by now well connected with the meritocracy of the rail industry and well schooled in all aspects of railway vehicles.

In 1905 Gresley became chief of the carriage and wagon department of the Great Northern Railway, responsible for everything that moved on the GNR (apart from the locomotives). This included responsibility for the East Coast Joint Stock carriages used on through trains to Scotland. He also became deputy to the Locomotive Engineer, Henry Ivatt (1851–1923), who had also started his career at Crewe.

Ivatt was forward-looking and had responded to the need for heavier and faster trains on the Great Northern by introducing the 'Atlantic' type of express locomotive to Great Britain. He once said: 'When a locomotive engineer makes an engine that is capable of pulling a church, he is at once asked to hitch on the school as well.' This remark would be well understood

Opposite:
'A Knight of the Iron Road' was the title given to Sir Nigel Gresley CBE on a cartoon drawn to mark his presidency of the Institute of Mechanical Engineers, 1936–7. He is shown here next to his namesake locomotive of the A4 class.

and acted on in due course by Ivatt's chosen successor, Nigel Gresley.

Gresley soon made his mark at 'The Plant' (as the railway works at Doncaster is known). Within a year, the first of his designs for carriages emerged, followed in 1906 by some coaches for the East Coast Joint Stock's new royal train. In 1907 Gresley unveiled a carriage design that is now commonplace worldwide for high-speed trains but which he pioneered in the United Kingdom. This used an arrangement whereby the bogie (or truck) under a carriage is shared by more than one coach body, giving a smoother ride at speed. Whilst beneficial for express trains, it also helped the Great Northern recycle old carriages. As a result, thirty years later the privileged few could enjoy elegant and smooth-running 'high-speed trains' out of King's Cross whilst commuters endured carriage interiors and layouts from the Victorian age.

Gresley was an apprentice at Crewe on the London & North Western Railway when express trains like this were running on the West Coast Main Line. Here Webb-designed locomotive *Jeannie Deans* is taking water at Bushey troughs in 1899 on a train to Glasgow formed entirely of corridor coaches.

Horwich works, where Gresley acquired a lifelong interest in locomotive and materials testing, a mark of his work when he moved to Doncaster.

These Doncaster-built coaches date from 1890 but lasted in service until 1946 owing to Gresley's championing of 'articulated' (shared) bogies, which were fitted to these carriages at Doncaster in 1908.

The 'articulated bogie' showed that Gresley, like his predecessor, Ivatt, was an engineer prepared to look at the best of what was available at home and abroad. Ivatt's 'Atlantics' were to stay in express passenger service on trains such as the 'Flying Scotsman' for over thirty years. They exemplified the advice given him by his own predecessor, Archibald Sturrock, that 'the power of an engine depends on its capacity to boil water'.

In 1911 Gresley succeeded Ivatt as the Great Northern's Locomotive Engineer. His first locomotive design featured Walschaerts valve gear, common abroad but a radical choice in Britain, and previously experimented with by Ivatt. During the First World War the Doncaster railway works was reorganised for the production of armaments; this work led to Gresley being made a CBE in 1920, and it also enabled him to plan for a more powerful engine to succeed the 'Atlantics'.

In the United States and in Europe good results had been achieved with the 'Pacific' wheel arrangement. This enabled a large boiler to be used, with the weight spread over twelve wheels. In 1914, the 'standard railroad of the world', the Pennsylvania Railroad of America, introduced a design of 'Pacific' express locomotive that had been developed by testing on their 'scientific' test plant at Altoona. Gresley, an enthusiast for scientific testing, was preparing designs for a 'Pacific' locomotive himself around this time and may well have seen the details when the magazine *The Engineer* featured the design in 1916.

Nigel Gresley's first design of locomotive, the GNR H2 class (later K1), was intended to be able to work both passenger and freight trains. Their lively ride at speed initially earned them the nickname 'Ragtimers' after the dance popular at the time.

In 1918 Gresley tried but failed to recruit Harold Holcroft from the South Eastern & Chatham Railway. Holcroft had worked out a satisfactory system for the valve gear of a three-cylinder engine, which Gresley favoured. With the right boiler, this would make for a smooth-running and powerful locomotive. Eventually Gresley designed his own version of Holcroft's valve gear to use on his 'Pacific' design.

Gresley's 'Pacific' featured three cylinders and the largest boiler possible on the Great Northern. By 1922 the design was ready and the Great Northern Railway's board authorised the construction of two locomotives. Given a good fireman, these locomotives (designated class 'A1') were well able to haul 600 tons at 50 mph, as intended. A further ten were authorised, and the third, number 1472, emerged from Doncaster works in February 1922 at a cost of £7,944. The following year this locomotive acquired the LNER reporting number of 4472 and the name *Flying Scotsman*.

At this point the Great Northern Railway became part of the London & North Eastern Railway, one of the 'Big Four' geographic groupings of railway companies created by government after the First World War. The 'Grouping' (1923) was a compromise to avoid direct state control (an idea that was spreading around the world) but it did not mean the companies were free of government interference. Freight rates were controlled at a time when road competition was growing, helped by government schemes such as the trunk roads programme, which turned the Great North Road into the A1.

In 1923 Gresley was appointed Chief Mechanical Engineer to the LNER and in 1924, A1 number 4472 was sent to London to promote their flagship express, now officially called the 'Flying Scotsman'. Gresley would go on to

The third of Gresley's new A1 'Pacifics', number 1472, leaving King's Cross in 1923. The following year it would find fame as *Flying Scotsman*, with the new number 4472.

Flying Scotsman alongside its one third scale working replica, Typhoon of the Romney, Hythe & Dymchurch Railway, at King's Cross shed in 1927. (The RH&DR was built as a miniature main line for two wealthy racing drivers and still runs today.)

Gresley stands next to his attempt to move steam technology forward, experimental high-pressure steam locomotive number 10000, known as the 'Hush Hush', at King's Cross station in July 1930. This was the only time the locomotive worked the 'Flying Scotsman' and proved hard work for the crew.

be responsible for the design of twenty-seven different classes of steam locomotive, including the most powerful in Britain and the fastest in the world, as well as electric trains. However, the A1 was not, initially, A1. Coal consumption was not as good as had been hoped for. At the British Empire Exhibition in 1924, near to *Flying Scotsman* was the Great Western Railway stand including a clearly smaller locomotive, *Caerphilly Castle*, which bore a sign proclaiming it to be 'the most powerful locomotive in the British Isles'.

Locomotive exchange trials the following year saw this point borne out by another GWR 'Castle' Class engine, *Pendennis Castle*, working trains from King's Cross. Lessons learnt from this exchange (backed up by a mild piece of industrial espionage) led to improvements, which brought a reduction in the A1's coal consumption from 50 pounds to 38 pounds a mile. This meant that theoretically an engine with a tender holding 9 tons of coal could work a train throughout from London to Edinburgh. The stage was set for a publicity coup that would be remembered long after steam trains had ceased to run on the route – London to Edinburgh by train, non-stop.

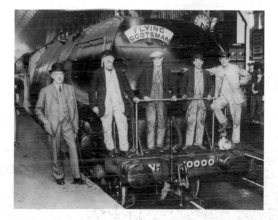

NON-STOP TO WAR

IN JANUARY 1928 Mr Eggleshaw, works manager at Doncaster, received an order for ten locomotive tenders of an entirely novel type. Designed to carry 9 tons of coal and 5,000 gallons of water, they included a corridor down one side which gave access to the cab from the train. (Some time earlier, Nigel Gresley's daughter had caught her father squeezing behind a line of chairs placed near a wall at their home, reportedly saying: 'If I can get through this, my biggest engineman can.') Fifty days later the LNER got its first 'corridor' tender. Attached to the right locomotive, this would allow the company to sidestep the 'eight-hour' rule and haul a train non-stop from London to Edinburgh.

But why do it? The LNER and its rival the London Midland & Scottish Railway (LMS) had an agreement about the speed of trains to Scotland. Running non-stop would not speed up the train unless this agreement was broken. However, in 1926 and 1927 there had been a large decline in passenger journeys, and during the General Strike in 1926 the London-bound 'Flying Scotsman' had been deliberately derailed. New, positive publicity for the 'Scotsman' was clearly a good idea. It would also be a grand team effort the length of the country, as each train would need two crews and the co-ordinated efforts of two hundred signalmen.

The new non-stop service was launched by the Lord Mayor of London, who declared that the train 'proves that British railways are not behind any others in the world... In fact, in the sphere of railway work they are always a little ahead of it.' (By then, as Gresley knew, some countries already had electrically powered express trains.) The rival LMS had run to Glasgow and Edinburgh non-stop a few days before as a one-off, but this barely dented the publicity the non-stop 'Flying Scotsman' received.

On 1 May 1928, at 10 a.m., with Driver Pibworth at the controls accompanied by Fireman Goddard and Inspector Bramwell, the 'Flying Scotsman' set off on its non-stop journey north. Crowds cheered as it passed whilst on board passengers could enjoy a meal in the 'all-electric' restaurant car, buy a newspaper, drink a cocktail, or visit Messrs B. Morris & Sons'

Opposite: Passengers on the 'Flying Scotsman' in the 1930s could not only have their hair done but could also visit the cocktail bar and try a 'Flying Scotsman'. The recipe called for whisky, vermouth, angostura bitters, sugar, syrup and ice.

The first non-stop 'Flying Scotsman' is ready to depart King's Cross station at 10 a.m. on 1 May 1928, hauled by number 4472 *Flying Scotsman*.

"THE FLYING SCOTSMAN"

FROM 1ST MAY
EDINBURGH
(WAVERLEY)
KING'S CROSS
WITHOUT STOP
392
MILES
CORRIDOR THROUGH TENDER
FRESH DRIVER AND FIREMAN
TAKE CONTROL WHILST
RUNNING

When the 'Flying Scotsman' started running non-stop in 1928, this poster helped to reassure passengers that the drivers would not get too tired.

Messrs B. Morris & Sons' barber shop on the non-stop 'Flying Scotsman' in 1928.

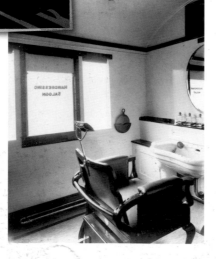

hairdressing saloon. Women could make use of the 'ladies' retiring room'. On its journey the locomotive would pick up water six times without stopping, using the then-common water troughs. Near Pilmoor number 2580 *Shotover* passed on the southbound train, carrying for the first time a headboard which read 'Flying Scotsman'.

Near Berwick, Charles Lake of the *Railway Gazette* visited the footplate with Gresley and proclaimed it all to be running smoothly. Arrival in Edinburgh was twelve minutes early, with the engine now worked by Gateshead men (Driver T. Blades and Fireman W. Morris) in the middle of a shift pattern that called for three nights away from home. On arrival, the crews were presented with inscribed pocket books and £10 (the result of a whip-round amongst the passengers). The story that a bearing on the

HORNBY

CLOCKWORK TRAIN

LNER
4472

Nº 44

Manufactured by
MECCANO LTD LIVERPOOL

The fame of *Flying Scotsman* was soon reflected in books, toys and countless other products. This is the artwork from Hornby's late 1920s *Flying Scotsman* train set. The locomotive inside the box bore little resemblance to that on the cover, though the artist has given *Scotsman* a shiny brass dome and green footplate and cylinders to make the difference less obvious.

tender had run hot near Edinburgh (cooled by Fireman Morris playing a hose on it) only came out later.

The non-stop era had arrived, as ever with the LNER, in a carefully managed blaze of publicity. From then until the Second World War, and for one season following it, the summer 'Flying Scotsman' was non-stop, with *Flying Scotsman* used to launch the first run of the service until 1936.

As hoped, the 'non-stop' attracted publicity and the LNER built on this. In June 1928 experimental radio equipment was fitted to the train to allow the passengers to hear the result of the Derby horse race. This was followed by a 'race' between a biplane and the train, with the passengers starting from the Savoy Hotel in London. Imperial Airways' aircraft *City of Glasgow*, with twenty-one people on board, had to refuel twice en route to Edinburgh from Croydon aerodrome. Despite the plane travelling faster, the train delivered its passengers to

The 'Flying Scotsman' derailed by striking miners at Cramlington, Northumberland, in one of the most notorious incidents of the General Strike of 1926. The volunteer crew on A1 number 2565 *Merry Hampton* and the 281 passengers escaped injury.

Edinburgh Waverley first, the plane's passengers being caught in traffic whilst driving in from Turnhouse aerodrome.

In 1929 British International Pictures persuaded the LNER to let it make a film called *The Flying Scotsman*. Completed just at the time the 'talkies' were coming in, from the third reel it had sound, the first British film to do so. The live action sequences

The fame of *Flying Scotsman* spreads, as this postcard from the 1930s proves. At this time Blackpool was rival 'Royal Scot' territory.

An Armstrong Whitworth Argosy airliner similar to Imperial Airways' *City of Glasgow*, which raced the non-stop 'Flying Scotsman', with maximum publicity, on 15 June 1928.

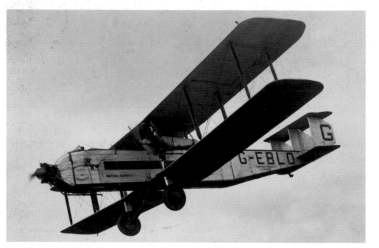

Actress Pauline Johnson alongside *Flying Scotsman* during the filming of 'The Flying Scotsman' near Hertford in 1929.

A 1930s table setting from the non-stop 'Flying Scotsman', epitomising the style and glamour of the era.

prompted the LNER to insist that the credits included a prominent statement to the effect that dramatic licence had been taken for film purposes and that the film did not represent the actual safety equipment used by the LNER.

Four expresses ready to depart from King's Cross station in 1930. Third from the right is the non-stop 'Flying Scotsman', hauled by Gresley A3 *Shotover*.

Flying Scotsman passes Hadley Wood on the 'Flying Scotsman' in December 1934. A little over a year later the locomotive lost its corridor tender and stopped hauling the non-stop 'Flying Scotsman'.

A SMART TURN OUT

CURTIS MOFFAT

" **THE FLYING SCOTSMAN** "

LEAVES KING'S CROSS LONDON
AND WAVERLEY STATION EDINBURGH
EVERY WEEKDAY AT 10 A.M.

LONDON & NORTH EASTERN RAILWAY

'A smart turnout', declares this poster for the 'Flying Scotsman' in 1935. Most of Gresley's A1s were named after winning racehorses, and the locomotive shown here was built as an A3, the development of the A1 design, and took the name of the winner of the 1931 St Leger, *Sandwich*.

Opposite bottom: *Flying Scotsman* displayed with appropriate headboard at a promotional event for the LNER at Ilford in June 1934. To the left is Gresley's latest locomotive, *Cock o' the North*, Britain's first express locomotive with eight driving wheels.

In 1932 the 'Flying Scotsman' took seven and a half hours for the run; the first of these speedier trains, driven by 4472's new driver, William Sparshatt, was waved off by the holder of the world land speed record, Sir Malcolm Campbell.

The *LNER Magazine* of January 1935 shows the moment 'Mr H. N. Gresley gives his congratulations to Driver Sparshatt and Fireman Webster at King's Cross station after their record-breaking 100 mph run from Leeds on 4472 *Flying Scotsman*'.

Streamlined A4 *Sea Eagle*, a sister engine to *Mallard*, pictured hauling the 'Flying Scotsman' near the Scottish border in 1938. Three years later, near here, the train was shot at by German fighter planes.

In the same year the artist Eric Gill designed his Gill Sans font for the LNER and took a footplate ride on the 'Flying Scotsman' as part of his fee. Gill noted that the train's luxuries contrasted strongly with the work on the footplate: 'Here we were carrying on as if we were pulling a string of coal trucks.' In the age of 'King Coal', when the jobs of locomotive crew were secure employment, few were likely to listen to Gill.

In 1934 the German Reich's diesel-powered 'Flying Hamburger' became the fastest scheduled train in the world. The LNER looked at buying a version of this but in the end Gresley was asked to design a luxury steam-hauled train

able to run from London to Newcastle in four hours. Design work included visiting the French locomotive-testing facility and a test run on which 4472 *Flying Scotsman* reached the magic speed of 100 mph – the first time this speed had been reached officially in the United Kingdom. Driver William Sparshatt (then aged sixty-one) had said to bystanders when leaving King's Cross: 'If we hit anything today, we'll hit it hard.'

A driver with his 'snap tin' and his fireman make their way through the corridor tender to take over the controls of the non-stop 'Flying Scotsman' in this publicity shot staged by the LNER.

Sparshatt's efforts with *Flying Scotsman*, Gresley's interest in streamlining (then in vogue), and the work of the French locomotive engineer André Chapelon, Gresley's friend, resulted in the A4 'Pacific', Gresley's masterpiece. These locomotives introduced the streamlined era to the East Coast Main Line and by 1936 had taken over running the 'Flying Scotsman'. The locomotive *Flying Scotsman* lost its corridor tender, as the engine began to work shorter distances on expresses out of King's Cross. Meanwhile, in 1938 A4 number 4468 *Mallard* achieved the world speed record for steam traction at 125 mph (the speed claimed at the time).

Mallard's triumph seemed to crown the great success of Gresley's working life. In 1932 the LMS had tried to recruit him, and in 1936 he had received a knighthood and an honorary degree. However, if the 1930s were a period of triumph for Gresley, they followed personal tragedy. In August 1929 his wife died from cancer at the age of fifty-four. Without his life partner, he concentrated on work, and as the 1930s ended in another world war he began to get bronchial and heart problems, but his work rate did not slow. He died in April 1941, two months after the unveiling of his last design, an express electric locomotive.

During the war the 'Flying Scotsman' train still ran, heavily overcrowded, and it was even shot at by German fighter planes near Berwick-upon-Tweed in 1941. In April 1943 *Flying Scotsman* the engine was painted in wartime black. Clearly the glory days were over.

The Spitfire *Flying Scotsman* of the Natal Squadron prepares for take-off at RAF North Weald on 4 May 1942. Paid for by the LNER and built at Castle Bromwich, this fighter plane saw active service over France and North Africa and was scrapped in 1947.

SOLDIERING ON

AFTER the mammoth and packed trains of the Second World War (often twice the length of today's trains and twice as slow), the poor maintenance, the dirt and the danger, peace returned to the East Coast Main Line. The 'Flying Scotsman' train ran one more summer non-stop. Change was in the air, and the non-stop service became the 'Capitals Limited', and then, in keeping with a new reign, the 'Elizabethan'.

Flying Scotsman the locomotive was given a much-needed overhaul in 1947, when it became almost the last of Gresley's A1s to be rebuilt with various refinements that improved their performance – a programme that had begun as long ago as 1928. The engine, regaining smart apple green paint, now bore a new designation, A3, to go with its new LNER number, 103, received the year before.

The LNER ceased to exist in 1948, the railways being nationalised along with the mines, steelworks and other major industries. A new corporate approach to the nation's railways included new paint schemes, and *Flying Scotsman* was repainted in British Railways' corporate livery, including for a short time 'express passenger blue', a striking contrast to LNER apple green. It was also renumbered again, and for the rest of its time in BR service it would carry the number 60103.

Meanwhile the 'Flying Scotsman' train received new coaches, including a new buffet in 'Festival of Britain' style, its 22-foot-long bar much remarked upon. Gone also was the teak exterior favoured by Gresley; instead, there was shiny painted steel, initially in a startling carmine and cream livery quickly nicknamed 'blood and custard'. People had a sense of an old order passing away, even though it would be the mid-1950s before the 'Flying Scotsman' would take less time for its journey than in the 1930s.

By 1953 the grand corporate vision for the nation's transport was beginning to slip. The government turned to General Sir Brian Robertson, who had organised the supplies to Montgomery's victorious Eighth Army, to sort it out. A 'Modernisation Plan' was soon unveiled, grand, forward-looking and, unlike the Eighth Army at El Alamein, ultimately doomed.

Opposite:
Flying Scotsman leaves Leeds in 1956, heading for London with the 'White Rose' express – a photograph by the Reverend Eric Treacy, at that time Archdeacon of Halifax.

A careworn *Flying Scotsman* pictured just after the Second World War. All LNER locomotives were renumbered in 1946 and *Flying Scotsman* became 103, the number seen here on the front buffer beam.

A poster for the 'Flying Scotsman' in 1950, after the non-stop era. Gresley's locomotives were now being replaced by those designed by his successors, Edward Thompson and Arthur Peppercorn.

THE
FLYING SCOTSMAN
WEEKDAYS

NORTHBOUND			SOUTHBOUND
dep 10 0 am	LONDON (KING'S CROSS)	↑ arr 6 0 pm	
dep 12A 6 pm	GRANTHAM	dep 3 56 pm	
dep 3ª19 pm	NEWCASTLE	dep 12 46 pm	
arr 5ª54 pm	EDINBURGH (WAVERLEY)	dep 10 0 am	
READ DOWN		READ UP	

BRITISH RAILWAYS

The aim was to overhaul Britain's railways completely at a cost of £1.2 billion. Despite the 'standard' (steam) locomotive-building programme then in full swing, steam would disappear as the country's railways moved into a 'modern' diesel and electric era. Trains would be quicker and cost less to run, whilst passengers, enticed away by the allure of the car (an increasingly affordable commodity), would be won back.

A few historic examples of the steam era would be preserved, overseen by the British Railways Board's new Curator, John Scholes, helped by suggestions from enthusiast bodies and from the regions of BR. The Assistant General Manager (Technical) for the Eastern Region, Terry Miller, who had been an apprentice under Gresley, suggested that he be represented by *Mallard* and fast freight locomotive *Green Arrow*. The star at the birth of the 'talkies', *Flying Scotsman*, was not on the list.

Meanwhile, increased leisure time boosted holiday traffic, but greater personal mobility was often achieved through the motorcycle and the car, whilst buses and lorries were slicing away regular freight and local passenger traffic. In 1958, well before anyone had heard of Dr Beeching, a complete 182-mile network in Norfolk and Cambridgeshire closed, to save £640,000. The last train on that line from Great Yarmouth ran with a placard tied to the front of the locomotive; it read: 'That's yer lot.' Within ten years it would be for many branch lines, and for steam-hauled trains on the national network.

By now a motorway building programme was underway and road traffic was growing to the point where Ernest Marples, the new Minister of Transport, was forced to introduce parking restrictions in towns for the first time in 1959. In that same year Captain Bill Smith RNR bought a former Great Northern Railway tank engine for an undisclosed sum, the first individual to 'preserve' a standard-gauge steam engine.

Smith's purchase neatly rounded off a decade when railway preservation had moved from a passive hobby (this was the heyday of trainspotting) into something more active. The Talyllyn Railway ran with volunteers for the first time in 1951; member number one of the world's first railway preservation society was the poet John Betjeman, later a campaigner against the wholesale destruction of the great monuments of the Victorian era such as Euston and St Pancras stations. Betjeman wrote in 1953: 'We "own" British Railways but we are allowed no say in them. We really do own the Talyllyn Railway. Perhaps its example will put life into the dead hand of British Railways and help save the remaining branch lines.'

British Railways was too busy trying to improve its services, including the 'Flying Scotsman', to notice this criticism. Diesels were being built and long-distance routes got new carriages designed to provide a splendid view, with windows that went down to only 25 inches above floor height. At the same time work went on to improve the ride quality of these coaches, helped by

A British Railways restaurant car from the 1950s. There is still silverware on the tables but the opulence of the 1930s has been replaced by the cautious styles of the 1950s.

The 'Elizabethan', Britain's last steam-hauled non-stop train, arrives at Edinburgh in 1953. The locomotive is A4 class 'Union of South Africa'.

The 1950s were the era of mass trainspotting. These aficionados watch the trains from the top of the Norman keep overlooking Newcastle Central station in August 1950.

a steady improvement of the track. Whilst steam faded away, the route of the 'Flying Scotsman' was being prepared for speed.

During the 1950s *Flying Scotsman* the locomotive was based for a time at Leicester but then transferred back to King's Cross shed, where the managers still had affection for the old girl. It was all a long way from 1938, when the fiftieth anniversary of the Races to the North had seen *Flying Scotsman* at the head of a new 'Flying Scotsman' train alongside an old-fashioned express of the Victorian era, hauled by the preserved Stirling 'Single'. That occasion had given rise to the first enthusiast railtour, an idea that returned in the 1950s helped along by the railway enthusiast Alan Pegler, a former dive-bomber pilot, now an industrialist based in Retford.

Pegler ran his first special train as an outing for his company, Northern Rubber, in May 1951 and the experience led him into organising trips for enthusiasts. In 1954 he helped rescue the Festiniog Railway. Pegler's enthusiastic promotion of railways eventually got him invited to join the Eastern Area Board of British Railways as an industry representative. This gave him an inside view of the turmoil that led from the grand vision of the Modernisation Plan to the trauma of the Beeching Report. It also gave him a chance to keep an eye on 60103 *Flying Scotsman*, a favourite of his since he had seen it at the British Empire Exhibition.

Flying Scotsman leaves Welwyn North Tunnel on 20 July 1959. By this stage the BR Modernisation Plan was bringing forward the diesel era – hence the graffiti scrawled on the tunnel portals either by rail staff anticipating redundancies, or by diehard steam fans.

Flying Scotsman enters Peterborough on the 'Tees–Thames Express' in 1960, running alongside a harbinger of the future, the prototype Deltic.

In the 1950s Britain's railways were beginning to struggle to maintain their importance as a mass carrier. Developments such as the new Mark 1 carriages, which passengers on the 'Flying Scotsman' enjoyed, with their carefully designed interiors and a décor that included polished and labelled rainforest woods, were an important part of the fight to maintain passenger numbers. In an era of mass employment, the fact that drivers were moving

In autumn 1958, at the start of the diesel era, a brand-new English Electric Type 4 locomotive, number D207, waits to depart King's Cross station on the 'Flying Scotsman'.

over to diesel locomotives, with roomy cabs, great views ahead and effortless power was also important. They were given smart diesel driver uniforms, enjoyed a day at the 'desk' (as they called the driver's control panel) and went home soot-free.

This was a transport revolution started before the Second World War, but delayed by it. In 1947 George Ivatt, the son of Gresley's predecessor on the GNR, produced Britain's first main-line express passenger diesel locomotive, featuring engines by English Electric. It would lead to the EE Type 4 (Class 40), a locomotive that would prove the worth of this kind of power, and in June 1958 one of these became the first diesel to work the 'Flying Scotsman'.

English Electric was then being run by Lord Nelson, a trained engineer and astute businessman. With the help of a retired rear admiral, he came up with a solution for a cash-strapped British Railways, which wanted more electrification but could not persuade the government to fund it – the 3,300-horsepower 'Deltic' diesel locomotive.

By 1961 the Eastern Region of BR, having lost out to the London Midland Region in the battle for money for electrification, got its first production Deltic. Roughly twice as powerful as the steam locomotives they replaced, these diesels would become, as one driver put it, 'boss of the job', once teething problems were sorted out.

In 1961 *Mallard* hauled the last steam hauled 'Elizabethan' and three years later *Flying Fox*, a sister engine to *Flying Scotsman*, appeared at King's Cross at the head of the 'Flying Scotsman' after a Deltic had failed – this was the last steam-hauled 'Flying Scotsman'.

A4 number 60014 *Silver Link* departs King's Cross station in 1950 hauling the 'Flying Scotsman'. Its condition is a long way from the silver and grey livery of the high-speed 'Silver Jubilee' service of the 1930s, which it inaugurated at 112.5 mph.

THE
FLYING SCOTSMAN

1862 - 1962

BRITISH RAILWAYS

BRITISH RAILWAYS

COAL TO CATENARY

IN 1956 a new diesel locomotive painted in a startling powder blue livery had started hauling trains in Britain. The locomotive used a novel 'opposed piston' high-speed diesel engine, lightweight and powerful, and represented a £250,000 gamble by the manufacturers, English Electric. Railway modernisation was already running into trouble and if passenger numbers were not to go into terminal decline, as was happening in the United States, and government would not fund wholesale electrification, then British Railways needed the Deltic.

On test the locomotive was remarkable and by 1958 the *York Evening Press* was excitedly writing of the possibility of trains from York to London taking only two and a half hours. When it was agreed to electrify the line from London Euston to Liverpool and Manchester, the Eastern Region quickly put together a business case for Deltics as a stop-gap. In 1958 an order for twenty-two Deltics was approved. They would replace fifty-five steam locomotives (including number 60103 *Flying Scotsman*) and all the paraphernalia that went with steam – coaling plants, water towers, maintenance crews with large spanners and flickering oil lamps, and heaps of ash.

In January 1961 Deltic number D9001, complete with design makeover and fetching two-tone green livery, arrived at Doncaster. In May, D9003 was on display at Marylebone station, just as *Flying Scotsman* had been in 1923. When the Eastern Region celebrated the hundredth anniversary of the 'Flying Scotsman' in 1962, in a conscious echo of the 1928 start of the non-stop runs, D9020 *Nimbus* was flagged away from King's Cross station by the Lord Mayor of London. The 'Flying Scotsman' train now managed the run in a headline-making time of six hours at an average speed of 65.5 mph. Carriages included a 'mini-buffet', as well as a restaurant car, as for the first time passengers would arrive in town well before supper.

Faster trains were made possible not just by the 3,300-horsepower Deltic locomotives but also by upgrades in the track. The post-war LNER was the first railway in Britain to try mechanised track maintenance, using a machine

Opposite:
The 1962 poster celebrating the centenary of the 'Flying Scotsman' prominently featured the brand-new 3,000 horsepower Deltic locomotive.

T5284

The prototype Deltic passes Potters Bar on a test train on the East Coast Main Line in 1959.

imported from Switzerland. Chief Civil Engineer 'Sandy' Terris's progressive track improvements produced lines designed for 100 mph for the first time. By 1973, 80 per cent of the route to Newcastle was passed for 100 mph and the 'Flying Scotsman' now took five and a half hours.

Higher speeds showed that a better carriage was needed, and a new design was developed, for the first time using computer modelling, as well as the French test facility at Vitry (once favoured by Gresley), to produce a smoother ride. By the end of the 1960s the Deltic-hauled 'Flying Scotsman' was formed of these Mark 2 carriages, complete with ergonomically designed seats made from moulded plastic with blue and black checked covers. New touches included individual lights, ashtrays in the arm rests, and toilets with hygienic foot pedals for the flush.

The first electric train from London to Liverpool in 1965. Once the money was committed to the electrification of the West Coast Main Line, the Eastern Region used Deltics to achieve electric railway timings on the East Coast Main Line.

Left: Workmen erect the 100 mph sign on the East Coast Main Line in Lincolnshire in 1964.

Below: The Deltic-hauled 'Flying Scotsman', sporting the diesel era 'winged thistle' headboard, passes through Retford station in June 1965, during remodelling of the tracks for increased line speeds.

By 1969 electric heating was introduced, and in 1970 the possibility of a journey of quiet contemplation was lost with the fitting of a public address system. In 1971 air-conditioning meant an end to arguments as to the amount of ventilation suitable for a pleasant journey. However, catering carriages were still BR Mark 1 vehicles with a lively ride and windows that opened to the elements. (With a smoking ban then unimaginable, perhaps this was for best.)

Stocking the shelves in the 'mini-buffet' of the 'Flying Scotsman' in July 1962 – a faster train but more workaday refreshments than in pre-war days.

Passengers enjoy the comfort of a new Mark 2 carriage on the inaugural run of the high-speed (Deltic-hauled) King's Cross to Newcastle service in May 1970, when armrest ashtrays were a useful innovation.

Whilst passengers flocked to the quicker trains, drivers appreciated the power of the Deltics and the fact that they had two engines at their control within the body of one locomotive. At first, though, crews might find that they had to switch from the clinical environment of a diesel cab to the harsh, hot surroundings of a steam cab at short notice as Deltic failures ran at up to 20 per cent in the first two years. Many failures were caused by the Deltics having small but troublesome steam boilers for train heating. In a further throwback to the steam age, these could be replenished using water troughs (although these had gone by 1969). When electric train heating was introduced, the distinctive smell of gently steaming horsehair (with which the BR Mark 1 seats were stuffed) was lost forever from the 'Flying Scotsman'.

In February 1970 Terry Miller, Chief Engineer, Traction and Rolling Stock for British Railways, proposed a new train to the BR board. This was another stop-gap to fill in before Britain could go over to widespread electrification and the high-tech tilting 'Advanced Passenger Train' (APT). The 'High Speed Train' (HST) was only two years in development but became the fastest diesel train in the world and is still in service on the East Coast Main Line.

British Rail attempts a return to stylish dining, as epitomised by this 1980s poster for 'Traveller's Fare' which features a celebrated East Coast Main Line location – the view from the Royal Border Bridge at Berwick.

1980s passengers enjoy the air-conditioned comfort of the Intercity 125 (HST). Commented on at the time was the fact that these services could be enjoyed without paying a supplementary fare.

When new, the HST's Mark 3 coaches redefined passenger comfort for a mass market. They were a good 10 feet longer than previous coaches, had air-conditioning as standard and ran smoothly at speeds up to and over 125 mph. Their interiors had double seats, either faced around a table or in ranks facing to the centre. The latter type had a fold-down tray and magazine rack, an increasingly familiar feature to a British population getting used to airliner interiors. Catering vehicles were included, which in the early years served beer on tap and a choice of red, white or rosé wine (the 'Flying Scotsman' cocktail now a distant memory). By 1983 (long before the mobile phone revolution), one could say 'I'm on the train' for the first time when on-train payphones became available.

The HST's distinctive buffer-less reinforced glass-fibre nose-cones, styled by industrial designer Kenneth Grange, were painted bright yellow and became a symbol of inter-city travel (enthusiasts nicknamed them

HST number 254012 passes Dringhouses near York in the late 1970s.

'Flying Bananas'). By 1979 the HST 'Flying Scotsman' took only 4 hours 37 minutes, with one stop at Newcastle.

If the drivers had liked the Deltics, they loved the High Speed Train. At last they sat in a quiet air-conditioned cab, with the ability to go up Stoke

The High Speed Train (HST) era at King's Cross station in the 1980s.

Bank as fast as *Mallard* had gone down it, and yet still stop at the signals (many in placements that dated to pre-war days). Today the HSTs have been re-engined but they remain, in terms of passenger comfort, the train by which all other British trains are judged.

In 1990, a good sixty years after it was first discussed, the East Coast Main Line was electrified all the way to Edinburgh. HSTs now shared express duties with trains hauled by Class 91 electric locomotives, whose designer, John Dowling, had worked on the Deltic. Capable of 140 mph, these clever 6,300-horsepower machines were a follow-on from the Advanced Passenger Train project and run coupled to Mark 4 carriages originally designed for tilting trains. In an age that favours under-floor engines spread along the train, they are likely to be the last express passenger locomotives built for the route. During their introduction, one Leeds to London train was reported to have descended Stoke Bank at 140 mph and in September 1989 one established the British locomotive speed record of 162.8 mph, again descending Stoke Bank.

A later test train managed King's Cross to Edinburgh in just under three and a half hours, an average speed of 112.5 mph, proving that the Class 91s provide a fitting final chapter to locomotive power on the route of the 'Flying Scotsman'.

Class 91 *Swallow* arrives at York with the first electric-hauled train service in 1991. Capable of 140 mph running, these locomotives have been restricted to 125 mph maximum as the East Coast Main Line still relies on lineside signalling. The train is partly obscured by the overhead catenary installed to electrify the route.

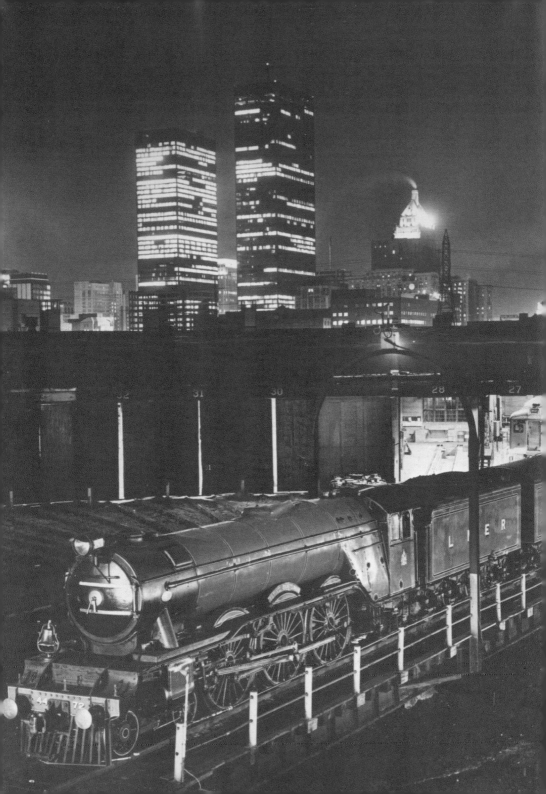

SAVING OUR SCOTSMAN

IN MAY 1962, when the hundredth anniversary 'Flying Scotsman' was waiting to depart from King's Cross station, by chance number 60103 *Flying Scotsman* was also there. A suggestion that the steam locomotive be parked alongside the Deltic was quickly dismissed; the railways wanted the future celebrated, not the past. Alan Pegler was also there and later recalled feeling sorry for the veteran steam locomotive. A year later, when a fund to 'Save our *Scotsman*' had not raised the asking price of £3,000, he bought the engine himself. The purchase gave the new Chairman of British Railways, moderniser Dr Richard Beeching, the excuse to sack Pegler from the BR board.

Pegler's purchase deal included use of a shed at Doncaster, access to the network (for a fee), plus work to return the engine to its British Empire Exhibition livery of LNER apple green. The most visible of the modifications of the previous forty years, a double chimney and German-style smoke deflectors, went, and *Flying Scotsman* regained a corridor tender and its old LNER number, 4472.

4472's first special train was for Festiniog Railway Society members; the route north was lined with sightseers. At Birmingham eight thousand people turned up to see the train. This would be the pattern from now on, the engine's preservation clearly having struck a chord with a public unsure of the amount of change the railways were going through. By 1965 the BBC children's television programme *Blue Peter* was declaring it to be 'the world's most famous locomotive'. When in 1968 it re-created the non-stop run of forty years before, television covered the event, using four helicopters and two camera crews.

In 1966 the engine acquired a second corridor tender to cope with a railway increasingly lacking water and coaling facilities, and by September 1968 it was the only steam engine allowed on the network. By then Pegler had determined on a new challenge, away from a railway that was often hostile to an operation that made the past seem glamorous: he would take *Flying Scotsman* to America.

Opposite:
Flying Scotsman
at Spadina
Roundhouse,
Toronto, in August
1970, halfway
through its
American
adventure.

Alan Pegler waves from the cab of *Flying Scotsman* as it leaves King's Cross station on its last run for British Railways (a train for Leeds) in January 1963.

Flying Scotsman on its first run as a privately owned engine in April 1963. The train took Festiniog Railway Society members to their annual general meeting. *Flying Scotsman*'s new owner, Alan Pegler, had helped rescue the narrow-gauge Festiniog Railway in the 1950s.

A trade mission, backed by the government and with the endorsement of Prime Minister Harold Wilson, set off in 1969. With *Flying Scotsman* went a locomotive crew provided by BR (and paid for by Pegler), and a nine-coach train which included two Pullman cars, a gift from the British government

Left: *Flying Scotsman* returns to King's Cross as a 'preserved' engine hauling a two-coach special for the Bassetlaw Division Conservative Association in October 1963.

Below: The re-creation of the steam-hauled non-stop run in May 1968 drew large crowds to King's Cross station and people to the lineside all the way to Edinburgh. A BBC documentary cemented the fame of this steam survivor at a time when Britain's scrap merchants were hard at work cutting up redundant steam locomotives.

Flying Scotsman passes Northallerton on 31 August 1969 already fitted with a bell for its forthcoming North American tour. After August 1968 *Flying Scotsman* was the only steam engine allowed on the British Railways standard-gauge network.

Piper Robert Crabb and other members of the tour team perform for the cameras in Philadelphia in 1969 on *Flying Scotsman*'s first American tour, dubbed 'Mission I' by George Hinchcliffe, the tour manager (on secondment from a school in Lincolnshire), a friend of Pegler.

to the US National Railway Museum, and an observation car converted into a pub. The train carried trade stands for twenty-one of Britain's largest exporting companies, from British Petroleum to BSA motorcycles and from Cutty Sark whisky to Pretty Polly tights; Watneys provided the beer.

The on-board team included 'Miss Flying Scotsman', a butler, a pipe major (who had played at Stalin's funeral), a Winston Churchill lookalike (in fact Churchill's nephew), and, courtesy of an accompanying promotion that soon folded, ten mini-skirted sales girls. Despite being shot at by IRA sympathisers when approaching New York, the tour was a success, with whole towns turning out to see the train and each stop co-ordinated with a 'Buy British' campaign in the local chain store. At Washington DC British Railways' chairman Sir Henry Johnson visited with the British ambassador. In total the 2,251-mile trip visited seventeen American states and was profitable, although not by enough for Pegler easily to afford to return *Flying Scotsman* to Britain.

A trip for summer 1970 was planned, the decision to run it helped by the fact that the US authorities had given Pegler permission to drive *Flying Scotsman* himself (something denied in Britain). However, this time there were no big companies and no government support. The train ran from Texas to Toronto, with Pegler having the time of his life, but losing his personal fortune.

Flying Scotsman at Carnforth depot in 1974. At this time 'Steamtown' at Carnforth was a visitor attraction and Scotsman was regularly to be seen hauling excursions from there.

In 1971, in an attempt to clear his debts, Pegler took the train to 'British Week' in San Francisco, a mere 3,300 miles away. With a scratch crew and a range of credit cards, Flying Scotsman made it to California, having by then done 15,400 miles in North America. Here the Scotsman circus finally hit the buffers after a venture to run a tourist service along the dockside proved a financial disaster. Pegler returned to Britain to file for bankruptcy; the engine went to an army base for safekeeping.

Wealthy railway enthusiast William McAlpine heard of the engine's plight and sent George Hinchcliffe, Pegler's US tour manager, to the States to put together a rescue deal. McAlpine, a director of the construction firm Sir Robert McAlpine Ltd (founded by the great Victorian railway builder 'Concrete Bob' McAlpine), was to own Flying Scotsman for twenty-three years, longer than any other individual.

In 1973, when Flying Scotsman returned from America, an estimated 100,000 people turned out to see it steam by. Here it arrives in Derby to cheers from the watching crowds.

Flying Scotsman at Marylebone shed in October 1986, reunited with fellow Gresley engines, A4 'Pacifics' *Mallard* and *Sir Nigel Gresley*.

Flying Scotsman arrives at Sydney in October 1988. Shipped to Australia on board the *New Zealand Pacific*, the locomotive was washed down regularly with clean water to protect the paintwork from the salt spray; by the time the ship made landfall in Australia water on board was rationed.

In February 1973 *Flying Scotsman* returned from the United States and ran under its own steam from Liverpool to Derby for repair, watched by an estimated 100,000 people. Its American adventure and the effervescent Pegler (by then busy lecturing on cruise ships to pay off his debts) had ensured that its fame had lasted beyond the steam age. Once repaired,

Flying Scotsman went back to hauling railtours as one of a number of steam engines now passed for main line running. In 1984 it even pulled the royal train with the Queen Mother on board.

In 1988 McAlpine was invited to take *Flying Scotsman* to Australia for the country's bicentennial celebrations. (The organisers had tried to borrow the steam speed record holder, *Mallard*, from the National Railway Museum.) McAlpine agreed to *Flying Scotsman*'s visit on the condition that a bond was put up that would ensure its return, no matter what.

In Australia (as in North America) the engine performed almost faultlessly to large crowds. It became the first standard gauge steam engine to visit Alice Springs, established a non-stop record for steam of 422 miles, and went to Perth, Western Australia, a journey that included the 297 miles of straight track, the world's longest 'straight'. In a remarkable echo of the past, *Flying Scotsman* was reunited, 9,000 miles from home, with expatriate GWR 'Castle' Class locomotive *Pendennis Castle*, the vanquisher of the A1s in the 1925 locomotive exchanges. After 28,000 miles and fifteen months away, *Flying Scotsman* returned to Britain, via Cape Horn, meaning that the locomotive has not only visited three continents but also sailed round the world.

'Bill' McAlpine once said: 'I never really thought of her as mine. I always felt she belonged to the nation.' Before the engine did belong to the nation, there was to be one more flamboyant, publicity-conscious individual owner, businessman Tony Marchington. Marchington bought *Flying Scotsman* for £1.45 million (the price including a set of Pullman coaches) in 1996.

When it worked on heritage railways in 1994, *Flying Scotsman* appeared in the condition in which BR had sold it as seen here on the Llangollen Railway. This work included running on 'driver experience' courses, where for a fee members of the public could drive the locomotive.

This followed a business venture, Flying Scotsman Railways, in which McAlpine and pop impresario Pete Waterman (a former locomotive fireman) had tried to exploit the opportunity that rail privatisation seemed to offer. It had run into trouble and *Flying Scotsman* was sold to clear the debts. By then the engine was in pieces at Southall, having spent the previous few years running on preserved lines. It was returned to its late BR condition, complete with double chimney and German-style smoke deflectors, and painted in British Railways Brunswick green livery.

Its return to steam, paid for by Marchington, took four years and cost far more than he anticipated. Finally, in July 1999, *Flying Scotsman* ran once again from King's Cross to York, watched by large crowds. In 2001 shares were sold in the operating company as Marchington sought to take more of a back seat in his relationship with this famous but costly machine. The new company had ambitious plans to create a 'Flying Scotsman Village' visitor attraction, but these never came to anything, and overall the operation did not cover its costs, despite an exclusive deal to haul the 'Venice Simplon Orient Express' luxury dining train. In 2004 the company put *Flying Scotsman* up for sale.

This time the National Railway Museum stepped in to buy *Flying Scotsman*, which many of its visitors had for years assumed it already owned. Fund-raising to cover the £2.2 million purchase price was helped by a smart promotional campaign and unfounded rumours that an American millionaire

Flying Scotsman finally made it into the Highlands and is seen here crossing Culloden Viaduct in November 2000 whilst hauling a luxury train for the royal gunsmiths Holland & Holland. In the following year the public were invited to buy shares in Flying Scotsman plc.

Flying Scotsman joins the National Railway Museum during Railfest 2004 (the major celebration of two hundred years of rail locomotion) after a successful fund-raising campaign to save it for the nation.

might buy it. With the public's contribution matched by the entrepreneur Sir Richard Branson, and backing from the National Heritage Memorial Fund and the National Lottery, Flying Scotsman was finally 'saved' yet again. The handover was announced on 5 April 2004, sixty-three years after the death of its designer.

In May 2004 Flying Scotsman arrived in York to open the celebrations to mark the two-hundredth anniversary of the steam locomotive, pushed past a large and admiring crowd by a former royal train engine. So today, when the 'Flying Scotsman' passes the National Railway Museum on its daily journeys between London and Edinburgh, it is passing the home of 'the world's most famous locomotive' – Flying Scotsman.

Flying Scotsman, now finally a part of the National Collection, is seen leaving Scarborough in August 2004. After Railfest in 2004 the engine ran for two more seasons before going into the works at the National Railway Museum for a comprehensive and costly overhaul.

INDEX